The Benjami

By Alan Gammon

A remarkable true story about a young family that left England more than 150 years ago, laid out a new village half way around the world and named it after their hometown in West Sussex.

Printed and published in Littlehampton West Sussex 2014

ISBN 978-0-9927921-0-7

© Alan Gammon 2014

First published 2014

Alan Gammon
8 Channel Keep
St Augustine Road
LITTLEHAMPTON
West Sussex
BN17 5NQ

Tel; 01903 714896
www.benjamin-gray.co.uk

Ordering Information:
For details, contact the publisher at the above address.

Printed in the United Kingdom by Print Plus, Littlehampton.

This book is dedicated to the memory of the
late Mr Stan Natrass

The Norman 'Plain Tub Font' that was used to baptise Benjamin Gray. It is still in use today at St James the Great Church. *Circa 11th Century*

Index

Introduction

October 7th 2014 marks the 176th anniversary of the day Benjamin Gray left England destined for Australia. This book is a compilation of snippets of information collected from various sources. In Littlehampton West Sussex very few people have heard of Benjamin or of his eventful life in Australia. Local historian Stan Natrass and I initially put together a few sheets of paper of very sketchy information but, over the past few years, this has increased to that which you are reading here today.

In 2009 I received a letter from Jeannette Allen, passed on to me by resident Ray Hook, informing me that there would be a 150th anniversary celebration of the naming of the township of Littlehampton in South Australia. As the mayor at the time I felt we should do something to join them and play our own part in the celebrations so, to this end, I sent them a parcel containing information about our town and decided to visit them on my already planned holiday to Australia.

Much work has been done over the past few years, and genealogist Tessa Raymond has carried out stringent research on both the family and the ship's log. Prior to 1837 registration of births, marriages and deaths were not as thoroughly certificated as they are today so we had to rely on the records held by the parishes.

As more information became available it seemed to bring Benjamin Gray to life, a man whose life progressively became almost unbelievable, and prompted many more questions that needed answering. We must bear in mind behind every good man is a good woman and Eliza Ann Emery Gray was no exception. A strong woman with a formidable determination that her husband would succeed can never be underestimated. I hope their story will go some way in inspiring young people of today to fulfil their own ambitions and do well in their own lives.

A website has been set up to enable you to be updated with any further information should it become available and to view additional pictures.

Alan Gammon

www.benjamin-gray.co.uk

19th Century British Politics

The early 1800's in Britain were politically very turbulent times and a hotbed of unrest. After the Battle of Waterloo in 1815, Napoleon was defeated, soldiers had returned home from the battlefields and were left without work and with no state benefit system to support them. Because of their injuries and disabilities some wandered the streets as paupers surviving on the goodwill of passers-by. As a result of the war the cost of living rose considerably.

In 1832 The Reform Act of 1831 was introduced, which had previously been thrown out by Lord Grey's Whig Government. The bill was restricted to men who owned their homes which had an annual value of £10, a lot of money at that time. In rural areas there were property qualifications, the result being only one in seven adult males received the vote. The Great Chartist Movement was very active and strong, holding large meetings where thousands of people gathered all over the country demanding votes for all men aged 21 as well as annual parliaments.

In the 1830's steam threshing machines were being introduced to the British agricultural industry reducing the need for labour and throwing many people out of work.

19th century Britain experienced a huge gulf in

economic wealth with the vast majority of the country living in extreme poverty. The cost of living became very expensive, making it a struggle for many to survive and the increasing gulf between the rich and the poor dramatically increased the crime rate.

Poverty, social injustice, child labour, harsh and dirty living conditions and long working hours were prevalent in 19th-century Britain. Dickens' novels may best illustrate this. The British government introduced deportation for minor crimes to relieve the pressure on the over stretched prison service where male convicts outnumbered women by six to one. Punishments for some crimes were considered too harsh so the judges called the lawmakers to find alternative sentences, transportation was therefore introduced. Some 165,000 people were deported over the course of 80 years, after their sentence many never returned to England and stayed. Some women even turned to prostitution to survive.

The Gray Family
Benjamin Gray was the second son born into a working class family. His father, a carpenter originally from South Stoke near Arundel and also named Benjamin, together with his wife Martha lived in a flint cottage in Church Street in Littlehampton, West Sussex. *(See p29)*.

He was baptised on the 17th June 1810 at St Mary's Church just across the road from where he lived *(see page 28)*. The font is Norman in origin, a plain tub type design made from stone around 1110 by A.K. Walker. *(See page 1)*. It is still in use in Saint James' the Great Church in East Ham Road.

Benjamin was one of eight siblings. They were John, 1808, Joseph 1812, Jane 1815, Sarah Anne 1819, Sophia 1821, William 1823 and George Adolphus 1827. Benjamin followed in his fathers' footsteps by becoming a carpenter.

The 1841 census showed the Gray family as living in Church Street at plot 186. The property is a grade 2 listed flint cottage with. a stone dated 1700 set in the front wall. *(See p29)*

At the age of 25 Benjamin married, by special licence, 28 year-old Eliza Ann Emery from Broadwater, Worthing, on 21st January 1836 at St Mary's Church where he had been baptised. Their son named Guildford Emery Gray, born on 26th September 1837 was also baptised at St Mary's on 5th November of that year. *(See pages 31, 32 & 33)*.

It is unclear what prompted the young Grays to take such a bold step as to leave their families and emigrate to Australia. Could it have been the political unrest in Britain or the desire to raise their family in a young country that offered plenty of work opportunity and a brighter future?

It may have been both, since in 1815 the existing Colonial government of South Australia decided to promote emigration from England and even offered to pay some people their fare and to help to set them up in business and on farms.

Australia needed to be developed and it carried what was described as a 'convict stain' they wanted to change. They achieved this by creating incentives which would attract business minded people.

Compared to Europe Australia had much to offer new settlers to encourage them to work hard and earn a living. Between 1815 and 1840 in excess of 58,000 people had emigrated to Australia, settlers who then also encouraged their friends and relatives back home in England to join them and to share in their prosperity. To help the gender imbalance women were encouraged to emigrate and some were offered assisted passage. These female emigrants predominantly worked as domestics and naturally helped the population to grow. Britain at this time was leading the western world in new technology and due to the industrial and political changes being introduced, British emigrants brought with them these skills, knowledge and experience which helped considerably in speeding up Australian development.

South Australia was the only Australian state to be settled entirely by free settlers and in 1861 granted restricted women's suffrage. In 1895 it became the second place in the world to grant universal suffrage (after New Zealand), and the first where women had the dual rights to vote and to stand for election.

The Journey
To set off on their long journey to Australia the Grays may have left Little Hampton, (as it was spelt at that time), for Worthing where horse drawn coaches departed daily for London. At this time a journey to London was rarely undertaken by working class people therefore a person would have had to have been extremely resolute in their desire to emigrate. During this period Little Hampton had coal coming down from Newcastle, timber from Scandinavia and sea trade between London and the south coast all arriving in the busy Port. The possibility existed that, as Benjamin was a local carpenter, he may have had friends on the ships that delivered some of his wood, friends who could have taken him and his family to London. Many ships

that left The Port of London were destined for Australia, stopping at Portsmouth Harbour before leaving the British Isles and would have been the most likely boarding point for the Grays however, on this particular voyage, they are on record as having joined the ship in London.

They left England on the 7th October 1838 on the sailing ship 'Resource', commanded by Captain W. Boyle with 117 adults and 94 children on board. The route followed the coast of France, Spain, Africa then Easterly around the Cape of Good Hope and straight on to Australia. It showed in the ship's record that Benjamin Gray arrived with his wife and child at Port Misery on 23rd January 1839.

The journey had taken 3 months and two weeks, and most of the passengers during the first few weeks suffered terrible bouts of seasickness. Due to the intense heat, travelling through the tropics was also known to be very difficult and added to the misery of the unseasoned voyager. On these long, arduous sea voyages passengers who did not survive the rigours of the tropics were tossed over the side of the ship. Fortunately the Grays survived the rigours of the journey.

The name Port Misery is said to have been chosen because when the first settlers landed, it had mosquito-infested swamps in the area which caused extreme discomfort to new arrivals. It had also been suggested the name described the unsatisfactory handling of goods at the site, proclaimed as a harbour in 1837. In 1839 the name was officially changed to Port Adelaide.

Arrival at Adelaide
For the first year following their arrival in Adelaide the Grays lived within easy reach of the city. Benjamin found work and is credited with making the lectern in St Peter's Cathedral, for which he was paid 8 shillings and 8 pence (8/8d), equivalent to $1 Australian dollar in today's money.

Word got around that a new village was being planned in the Barker Hills and a great deal of carpentry work would be required. Captain Collet Barker had only discovered Mount Barker in 1830 just prior to being killed by Aborigines in 1831. Captain Charles Sturt named the area Mount Barker when he founded it in 1834, just 5 years before the Prussian Lutheran immigrants arrived. Prussian Lutherans were people who refused to join the Prussian Union of churches after a decree by King Fredereick William III of Prussia to publish a new service book for the Lutheran and reformed congregations. This was not well received and prompted some to flee their country for the USA, Canada and Australia. Religious refugees represented the first major wave of German settlement in Australia some of whom were active as missionaries and explorers. German immigrants formed the largest non-British European ethnic group in Australia.

Hahndorf

Hahndorf (Hahns Village) was named after Captain Dirk Meinhertz Hahn, who took German immigrants from Hamburg in his sailing ship 'Zebra' to Port Adelaide, and initially provided the funds for the new German settlers to purchase the land. The first Lutherans to come to Australia in any significant number were from Prussia and arrived in 1838 with Pastor August Kavel. Benjamin went to see if any work was on offer and found they needed carpenters so he moved his family within easy reach of the village to Blakiston where they gradually made many friends. The owner of the *German Arms*, Gottfried Lubasch, diversified to become a full-time farmer and consequently leased the hotel to James Ide and his wife. Sarah Hopkins Ide originated from East Wittering in West Sussex, where their family had run the George public house for over 50 years. Coincidentally Benjamin had occasionally frequented the George thus becoming friends with them in England and rekindling their friendship in Hahndorf.

As a result of Germany's involvement in the First World War, Hahndorf was renamed *Ambleside* after the Ambleside Railway Station but in the 1930's it reverted back to its original name.

When Captain Hahn sailed his final journey to Australia and retired from shipping he went to live in Hahndorf, by which time the villagers were settled, successful farmers and some even went to work for other landowners in the area.

Time moved on and the Gray family grew by two, with Sarah Elizabeth born in 1844 and Alice born in 1846.

In 1849 Benjamin and three friends latched on to the idea of building a village for themselves. He persuaded Francis Robert Hunt, his partner in a livestock business, and two other fellow St. James' parishioners to join him in laying out a new village on both sides of the Great Eastern Road.

Littlehampton South Australia
Situated just a few miles North of Hahndorf, Blakiston, the new home of the Grays, lies 3km west of Mount

Barker and is approximately 400m above sea level on the main Melbourne to Adelaide road. Blakiston was settled many years before with an inn and staging rest place for the mail and passenger coaches.

When friends Mr. Thomas Biddle a farmer, Francis Robert Hunt a brewer, John Smith a surgeon and Mr. John Forster all of Mount Barker, joined together to purchase the land required for their enterprise in three parcels, 5011 acres, 6010 acres and 5008 acres. In 1849 where the farms met they subdivided a portion of their respective land for which they received land grants and within two years these men had worked together to found the new village. By 1851 the village of Little Hampton was laid out but not officially registered until 1859. It is thought that each of the four landowners put their suggestion of a name into a hat and Little Hampton was drawn.

Before the public house was built in Mount Barker, Blakiston Hall (*See page 34*), became the original Grays' Inn, Benjamin's final settling point and where he and Eliza raised their family. Prior to opening a brewery he used the cellars under Blakiston Hall to brew beer, he also produced his own malt. Malting is the work of a maltster, being a mixture of sugars and is produced from cereal grain that, in the early days of germination, assists the growth of the new shoot. Barley was the most common grain used. It is moistened for a couple of days to produce a small amount of malt prior to the grain germinating then it is heated to dry the grain and stop germination. The grain is then mashed and the malt is extracted, baked and subsequently used.

He built the Union Hotel and St James's School. Samuel Stock and George Morphett donated land by deed to enable the formation of a board of trustees in order to build the St James's Anglican Church and rectory. The church board consisted of Francis Davison, Allan MacFarlane, Henry Seymour, George Fredrick Dashwood and John Finnis. The foundation stone was laid on October 3rd 1846, by Mrs. Davison with her husband Captain Francis Davison R.N. They commissioned Benjamin Gray to build the church and paid him from subscriptions. Accompanied by fellow carpenter Walter Simpson they completed the carpentry work. Benjamin was a devout member and attendee listed as a seat holder, and he later became a trustee and a Synods man of the church. The church still stands today and is one of the oldest in the territory. Walter Simpson incidentally was an Englishman, who stole six loaves of bread in Battersea in South London and was tried at the Surrey Quarter Sessions on 17th July 1818, where he was sentenced to seven years transportation to Tasmania. He had a chequered history in Australia and after being released from prison he married, left Tasmania and kept to the straight and narrow. He eventually relocated with his family to Adelaide. Simpson was a blacksmith, carpenter and bullock team driver so was very useful to Benjamin. He died in Blakiston on 17th Jan 1876 aged 75 years.

Among the many skills acquired by Benjamin were carpentry, surveying, brewing, Clerk of the Works and resident JP. In 1853 he stood for election as a rate payer and subsequently became a member of Barker Hills District Council and later Chairman of the Council.

On the 29th August 1879 the local press reported that *'Benjamin Gray JP brewer of Mount Barker, was standing on a platform in his brewery yesterday when by some means it gave way, precipitating him into a vat of scalding water. Fortunately he managed to catch hold of a beam and thus save himself from injury above the knees. Dr Weld was in attendance and tended to the injuries.'*

Sadly, Benjamin died of his injuries in Blakiston Hall six days later on the 3rd September and was buried in plot D1 at St James's Anglican Church cemetery on the 5th September 1879.

Pioneer Settlers

Benjamin Gray and the many other intrepid pioneer settlers of that time were the forerunners of the Mount Barker area and of today's modern Australia. The building of these villages played a huge part in the subsequent development of modern communities, creating employment, cultivation of the land and produce to openly trade.

South Australia was a colony to the British government, and the South Australia Colonisation Act of 1834 ruled that 802,511 square kilometres be allocated to non-convicts. The plan for the colony was to have no religious discrimination or unemployment. The new settlements were built on Kangaroo Island and were predominantly to the east of the province. By 1836 as it had a port, the focus was on the Adelaide area in particular Holdfast Bay and Glenelg.

Most of the other colonies had been founded by governors with near total authority, but in South Australia power was initially divided between the governor and the resident commissioner, so that government could not interfere with the business affairs or freedom of religion of the settlers.

Benjamin Gray's Family

Benjamin Gray senior was born in 1778 and married Martha Boxold on the 24th February 1805 at South Stoke Church near Arundel and died at Worthing in 1843 Martha succeeded him until 1871 when she also passed away.

Guildford Emery Gray the only son of Eliza and Benjamin was born in England in 1837, and Elizabeth Chapman was the mother to their two children, Francis Edgar Chapman Gray born on 23rd June 1861 and Eva Amelia Chapman Gray born on the 1st June 1864. Less than a year later Guildford obtained a special licence to marry Sylvia Warland on the 6th April 1865, but they were childless. In 1888 Guildford went to live in Broken Hill in New South Wales and established the Waverley Brewery in Silica Street with his friend Theodore Bruce who became the general manager with Guildford being the brewer. He died at Blakiston on the 20th June 1905 and the brewery closed in 1909. Elizabeth died on the 8th September 1912 aged 68 years at Blakiston. Sylvia died in 1932 aged 92. *A diagram of the family tree can be found on page 36.*

Eliza Emery Gray the eldest daughter to Eliza and Benjamin, was born in 1840 and married William Henry Taylor on the 29th June 1876. She died in 1892, they had no children. Sarah Elizabeth Gray their second daughter, was born in 1844, and died as a single woman at the age of 68 on the 8th September 1912. Alice Gray their youngest daughter, was baptised on the 23rd August 1846 at Nairne Chapel, Alice also died as a single woman aged 54 on the 22nd February 1901.

The Link with West Sussex

Contact with the two Littlehamptons, as far as we know, goes back to the Second World War when the primary school in Littlehampton South Australia sent food parcels to a school in Littlehampton England to help with the food shortage. In 2009 Littlehampton South Australia celebrated 150 years of the naming of their village. Throughout the winter From April to October they held many events from history days to conducted walks and tours. With the assistance of the Lord Mayor of Adelaide Michael Harberson, Mayor Ann Ferguson of Barker Hills District Council and the Littlehampton Community Association who arranged our visit during their celebration period.

Littlehampton was waking up to a light frost in the darker months of the year. We initially arrived at the Platform One Heritage Farm Railway, a brilliant local attraction also incorporating a museum and run by Glenn Liebelt and his family. On entering the pleasant, cosy reception we were greeted by people from the community. We settled down to coffee, biscuits and scones and chatted with the headmistress from the local primary school, members of the community association and many more who made the time to greet us. We took a trip on the miniature railway, the engine driven by Glenn followed by his faithful ewe named Sally, who is probably one of the tamest sheep in the land.

On our return we enjoyed a tour of the railway museum, where we could have spent all day absorbing the history of railway life.

To our surprise, a tour in a white Rolls Royce had been prearranged chauffeuring us around the village to interesting sites where we walked in the footsteps of the remarkable man, Benjamin Gray.

Shady Grove Church, stands alone among trees and is one of the oldest and the smallest churches in South Australia. It once had a dual purpose of being a school classroom during weekdays and a church at weekends. Classrooms of the 19th century were required to be heated by an open fire, and this is said to be the only surviving school classroom in Australia fitted with a fireplace. The interior is original and left much to the imagination, a gem of a building that earned its place in local history and still has the original row of coat hooks on the wall used by the children and parishioners.

St James's Anglican Church, a wonderfully well preserved building has beautiful stained glass windows. We walked around the back of the church and saw what is described as early graffiti etched in the exterior wall.

A short walk took us to Benjamin's' grave where the white marble cross stood proud inside a high curb inscribed by the names of his family featured in this book. We visited his home Blakiston Hall which is now occupied by a young family who kindly opened it for the first time for us to view. A peaceful house that gave the visitor a feeling that it was soaked in history.

At lunchtime we enjoyed eating at the Great Eastern Hotel, the bar, sporting a beautiful mural of a picnic at the races is one of its finer features. Our visit to the Littlehampton Brick and Paving Co provided a trip back in time to the Victorian era by viewing the old brick kilns. Awesome and very satisfying that that they had survived the rigours of time to allow future generations to learn how bricks were made. With hard hat on, a guided tour around the modern brick plant followed, where we watched the fascinating process of the clay being cut and forged ready for baking and loaded onto the lorries for delivery. Littlehampton Primary School was our next visit, the children showed us their work and asked many questions.

The afternoon came to an end with a visit to the Barker Hills District Council offices to meet the staff and to witness a citizenship ceremony for around thirty people. We proceeded to the council chamber and were seated next to local Member of Parliament Mark Goldsworthy. Mayor Ann Ferguson welcomed everyone, and delivered a wonderful speech, an eloquent overview of why we are all there, some reasons why people wanted to be citizens and what a fine decision they had made to want to be a part of Australia. The ceremony progressed for each person to individually be asked to come forward in front of the mayor, take their oath, receive a bag of goodies and a Banyan Tree to plant in their garden. The mayor, while handing them their citizenship certificate, said "Welcome to the finest club in the world", a very proud moment indeed for the recipients. It was heartening to see people fulfilling one of the most important decisions of their lives. Most of them had emigrated from England to Australia during the 1950s and 60s for just £10 through the assisted passage scheme. They raised their children as Australians and for some, two generations later decided to take up citizenship. Finally, I was required to make what was probably the most difficult speech I have ever delivered at the end of which, much to my surprise, I was made an Australian citizen – but only for the day!

In the evening we were wined and dined at Chappies Restaurant. Which was full of invited people from the community, including local councillors and our hosts who had escorted us during the day. The gathering was increased as local residents dropped in for a chat regarding the celebrations.

Toward the end of the evening the owner of the vineyard at Hahndorf presented me with a bottle of fine locally produced wine. A day to truly remember and most importantly a day that helped to reinforce the relationship between our towns. The preparation work in arranging the visit was greatly appreciated and was very special to both our towns.

Benjamin Gray, a figure from our distant past seemed to come to life for us during this heart-warming visit. So many people in Australia knew so much about him and yet so few in Littlehampton West Sussex had ever heard the name. On my return to England, to fulfil the wishes of the mayor and the people I met during the visit, I did what I could do to bring to the attention of our residents the history and achievements of this Littlehampton man who had lived such an interesting life so many years ago.

The Littlehampton Gazette carried a full page report and Littlehampton Museum held a small exhibition showing souvenirs and publications of the village from September 2009 to the New Year. Subsequently for more than two years since the visit I was asked by local community groups and clubs to give a presentation of this remarkable story. People listened with great interest and their many questions showed their genuine interest in the life of Benjamin Gray.

Littlehampton West Sussex Today

Littlehampton West Sussex is on the south coast of England, a small port situated at the estuary of the River Arun, it has a population of around 30,000 and dates back to Saxon times. A popular coastal destination town for day-trippers and tourists, it has a vibrancy of its own, a town that has developed from a seaside resort to a place where people want to live and to raise their families.

Largely developed, Benjamin Gray would find little now that would be familiar to him beyond the flow of the lovely River Arun which still threads its way around the town and past the site of the old timber yards which formed part of his trade. The east bank is now, for the most part, tastefully developed and the town still offers good ale houses, restaurants and a vibrant community. Beyond the confines of the town itself, beautiful walking countryside to the north and the west with a large and diverse population of flower and fauna. The west bank and the sandy west beach is largely unchanged with the remnants of the old boat building industry still visible and thriving with a marina filled with holiday boats, yachts' and small sail boats.

In the town there is a recently established weekly market and the town holds many entertaining events for young and old alike. Family Fun Days, a Town Show, carnival, bonfire night and an Armed Forces Day. The town has a museum and, recently, Commando Unit 1X Group of Royal Marines were given the freedom of the town in recognition of their services during World War Two. Littlehampton is believed to be the town where Ian Fleming organised his special commando group that possibly spawned the idea for James Bond.

New housing developments will continue over the coming years and regeneration is always high on the local council's agenda.

Littlehampton South Australia Today
Littlehampton has a population of over 2000 situated in the Adelaide Hills. It has a voluntary fire service and the village still commercially cultivates subterranean clover appropriately named 'Mount Barker'. Littlehampton Bricks are still made and sold as far afield as Japan. On the second Saturday of every month the market operates in the Memorial Hall and has around 25 stalls and claims to have something for everyone.

For children wishing to learn about farming, Platform One Heritage Farm Railway is the place to visit and they can enjoy a ride on the miniature train.

In 2008 the Littlehampton Community Association (LCA) restored Benjamins' grave, which was in a serious state of disrepair with no decendants in the district to care for it. Jeannette Allen was the special Projects Officer who made grant applications and with the personnel involved, priced up and dealt with quotes.

A successful application resulted in a grant from the History South Australia Cemeteries Trust, which helped to pay for the restoration. Volunteers Ray Allen, Peter Rayner and Rod Stone worked very hard to clear the grave site and were supervised and assisted by a local tradesman Klaas Van Donderen who professionally did the brick and concrete work, he also generously gave his time and supplied the concrete at no cost to LCA. Ray and Jeannette's border collie Harley also helped to supervise the whole operation.

For a very expensive headstone refurbishment by a heritage stonemason, the LCA raised funds through activities such as the monthly Country Markets and raffles. The LCA now has the responsibility of maintaining the grave site. Littlehampton won a Local Heritage Award for carrying out the restoration. *See page 38.*

Littlehampton Church 1791 (S H Grimm)
Courtesy of the British Library

The flint cottage, Church Street *circa 1700*

29

The last line above reads: June 17th, Benjamin son of Benjamin and Martha Gray

First line; Mary Anne Weller's name also appeared in Benjamin and Eliza's
entry in the marriage register. See page 32.

Benjamin Grays' baptism record
Courtesy West Sussex Record Office

The special marriage licence
Courtesy West Sussex Record Office

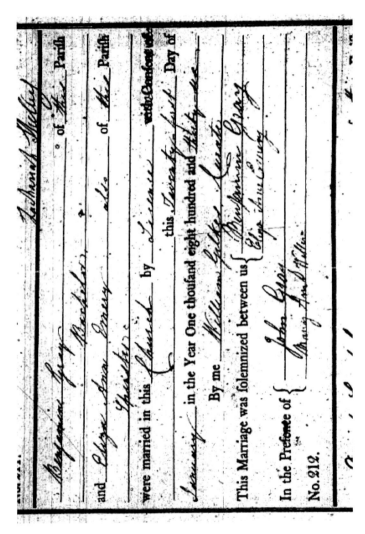

Parish register marriage entry
Courtesy West Sussex Record Office

32

Guildfords' Baptism record also showing his date of birth.
Courtesy West Sussex Record Office

33

Blakiston Hall was built close to St James' Anglican Church

Celebrating the 150th anniversary of the naming of the village.
Left to Right - Glenn Liebelt (LCA member), Ray Allen (LCA member), Jeannette Allen Secretary (LCA), Janet Pengilly (LCA committee member), Sue Harris (St James Cemetery Curator), Mayor Ann Ferguson (District Council of Mount Barker), Penny Rodgers & Alan Gammon.

35

The Gray Family Tree
1778-1932

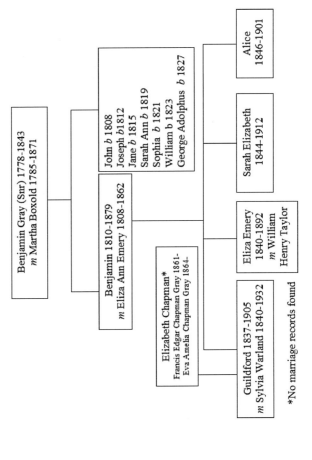

Benjamin Gray (Snr) 1778-1843
m Martha Boxold 1785-1871

Benjamin 1810-1879
m Eliza Ann Emery 1808-1862

John *b* 1808
Joseph *b* 1812
Jane *b* 1815
Sarah Ann *b* 1819
Sophia *b* 1821
William *b* 1823
George Adolphus *b* 1827

Alice
1846-1901

Sarah Elizabeth
1844-1912

Eliza Emery
1840-1892
m William
Henry Taylor

Elizabeth Chapman*
Francis Edgar Chapman Gray 1861-
Eva Amelia Chapman Gray 1864-

Guildford 1837-1905
m Sylvia Warland 1840-1932

*No marriage records found